FOLKESTONE
IN
50
BUILDINGS

PAUL HARRIS

AMBERLEY

First published 2016

Amberley Publishing, The Hill, Stroud
Gloucestershire GL5 4EP

www.amberley-books.com

British Library Cataloguing in Publication Data.
A catalogue record for this book is available from the British Library.

ISBN 978 1 4456 6374 6 (print)
ISBN 978 1 4456 6375 3 (ebook)

Typesetting and Origination by Amberley Publishing.
Printed in Great Britain.

Contents

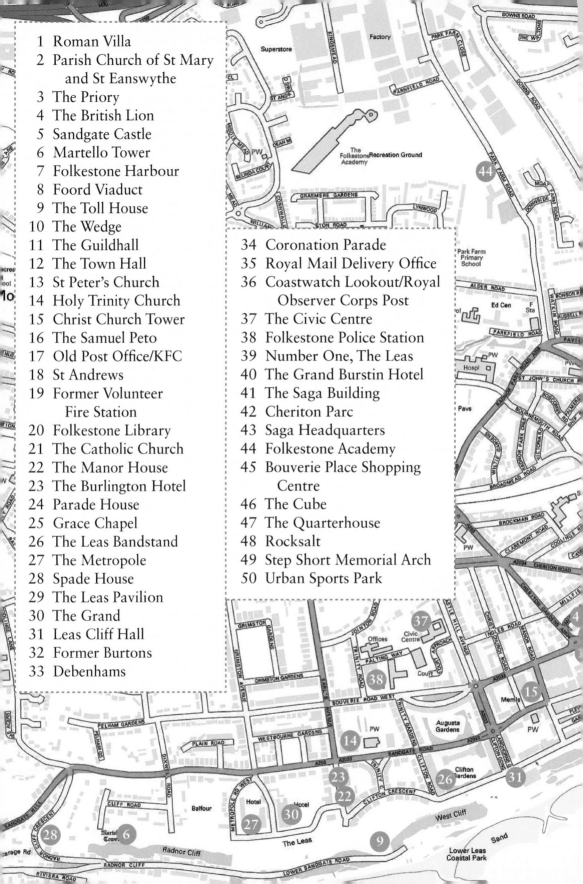

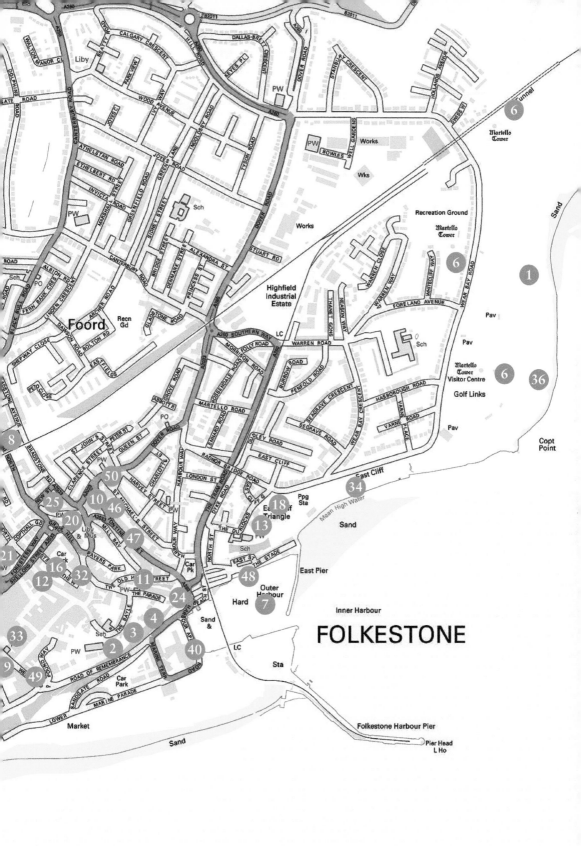

Introduction

The origins of Folkestone as a settlement are lost in prehistory, but the town's name perhaps gives us a clue. From the Iron Age until the eighteenth century, a stone quarrying and exporting industry flourished here. This seems to have commenced with 'quern' (milling) stone manufacturing and exporting from East Wear Bay from around 700 BC, until the end of the Roman period. Large greensand blocks were, however, collected from the cliffs between Hythe in the west and East Wear Bay to the east for centuries afterwards and exported for use in large-scale stoneworking – the harbour walls for instance.

A Roman presence was evidently established on the East Cliff area and at East Wear Bay, though this settlement seems to have faded out, leaving the fishing village near the current harbour to develop into today's town. This process went through a number of stages marked in a physical sense by the surviving buildings to be found around Folkestone. There was the establishment of a castle and monastic centre on the cliffs above the fishing village, and legend tells us that England's first nunnery was active here, its first abbess being Folkestone's patron saint, Eanswythe.

Folkestone during medieval times consisted of what we now think of as the 'old town' until it really took off with the establishment of the harbour, the coming of the railway, the commencement of cross-channel services to Boulogne, and the recognition by the major local landowner that this place had potential to become a high-class resort.

In the early nineteenth century, the Lord Radnor of the time employed architect Sidney Smirke (who designed the British Museum and its Reading Room) to plan a number of ambitious schemes, including the laying out of the West Cliff estate that became the fashionable Leas and West End of Folkestone. So many of the town's most notable and attractive buildings date from this time and from the rapid developments that followed thereafter.

Folkestone probably reached its most recent peak of prosperity early in the twentieth century when The Grand was built as 'gentleman's apartments', which were used regularly by the visiting King Edward VII and his mistress, Alice Keppel; Lord Radnor's 'policemen' patrolled The Leas to ensure good behaviour, and H. G. Wells was busy penning his most famous work just down the hill in Sandgate.

Since the early twentieth century, there have been many changes. The First and Second World Wars both profoundly affected the town. The decline of the traditional seaside holiday from the 1960s onwards, the development of the roll-on-roll-off car ferry service in the 1970s, the coming of the Channel Tunnel in the 1990s and the unfolding regeneration plans of the early twenty-first century have all left their mark, and most obviously in the buildings constructed in each period.

They all have a story to tell, not only about the buildings themselves and their architectural styles but the times they illustrate, the broader sweep of history – albeit in a local context. Then, of course, there are all the people who designed, built, worked, lived in or visited them; they all have their story.

In this book I shall move through Folkestone's history, illustrating its phases and changes as evidenced by fifty examples of its built environment from the earliest times to the second decade of the twenty-first century. My aim and hope is that this will help expand and clarify an understanding of this town and its history and therefore encourage its appreciation by both visitor and resident alike.

Paul Harris
Folkestone, September 2016

The 50 Buildings

1. The Roman Villa (*c.* AD 100), East Wear Bay, CT19 6PU

A busy industry manufacturing and exporting quernstones seems to have been operating at East Wear Bay from around 700 BC. The earliest substantial building for which we have any detailed knowledge is the Roman Villa that occupied a prime site on the clifftop at East Wear Bay.

This palatial building appears to have been established around AD 100, some sixty years after the Roman conquest under Emperor Claudius. This villa was occupied until around AD 70. The reason for its apparent abandonment then is not known but could be connected to the expectation of an imminent assault by Roman Imperial forces to bring an end to a decade of unilaterally declared independence by Britain, Gaul and Spain. Around this time all over the country, coins and treasure were hoarded away, possibly in anticipation of an imminent period of unrest and dislocation.

Whatever actually happened, the Roman Villa at Folkestone seems to have remained uninhabited, and it fell into a ruinous state for the next eighty years or so after which it was partially demolished and the site used for some, as yet unidentified, industrial or agricultural use for a further period, possibly into the early fifth century (AD 400–25).

The Roman Villa at East Wear Bay as it may have looked AD *c.* 250.

Above: Detail of the Roman Villa buildings as they may have appeared AD *c.* 250.

Below: Roman Villa excavations at East Wear Bay, 2012.

Over time, what was left of the building vanished from sight, no doubt due to its building materials being 'robbed' and used elsewhere until rediscovery in 1923 by schoolteacher S. E. Winbolt. His excavations opened up the site to public view until 1957 when it was covered over to protect the remnants of the structure from weather and vandalism. Further investigative excavations were carried out in 1989 by the Canterbury Archaeological Trust (CAT) and for several summer seasons from 2010 by the A Town Unearthed (ATU) project and CAT.

On each occasion, the site was open for members of the public to view the foundations and work in progress. At the time of writing, archaeological research and excavation is ongoing.

2. The Parish Church of St Mary and St Eanswythe (1138), Church Street, CT20 1SW

There has been a Christian community in Folkestone since AD 630 when King Eadbald of Kent had a church and convent built for his daughter, Princess Eanswythe.

Eanswythe, according to legend, had from her infancy 'renounced worldly pomps' and is said to have 'trod underfoot the treasures of this world'. As a teenager she turned down an offer of marriage from a Northumbrian prince in favour of a nun's life. Her convent became the first nunnery in England. She is also said to have performed many miracles in her time, such as forbidding the birds to eat the crops of the local people, curing the blind and lame and making water run uphill and across another stream 'unmingled' to supply her

Parish Church of St Mary and St Eanswythe.

Reliquary at the shrine of St Eanswythe.

Victorian restoration of Town Cross in the churchyard of St Mary and St Eanswythe.
Inset: Detail of the ancient top to the otherwise restored Town Cross.

nunnery. The latter, it has been suggested, is based on an early aqueduct system that, as the Town Dyke, supplied the 'old town' with fresh water until the nineteenth century. This may have been constructed or brought back into use in Eanswythe's time or later, in the twelfth century, and dedicated to her as she was by then recognised as Folkestone's patron saint.

The current church was founded and so dedicated by the then Lord of the Manor William d'Averanches in 1138, though most of the building dates from 1195 onwards. After a period of mixed fortunes, extensive improvements were made to the church by the canon Mathew Woodward between 1851 and 1898. Much of the variety and beauty that we see today dates from Woodward's tenure and is very influenced by his 'High Church' beliefs.

In 1885, the relics of St Eanswythe were discovered and placed in a shrine near the altar, where they remain to this day. An historical investigative project entitled 'Finding Eanswythe', which aims to examine and date the relics and search for evidence of her miraculous watercourse, has recently been set up by the Folkestone People's History Centre (FPHC).

In the churchyard is a Victorian replica of the Town Cross topped with much older work. Here, from 1313 when Folkestone was first granted a charter, the town's officials would meet every September to elect a mayor, a bailiff and twelve jurats.

Today the parish church, in addition to its normal services, hosts a number of exhibitions and concerts that bring in visitors who would otherwise be unaware of the beautiful interior of this church.

The priory in The Bayle today.

3. The Priory (c. 1425), 1/2 The Bayle, CT20 1SQ

The hilltop enclave known as The Bayle is among the oldest parts of the town. 'Bayle' means 'castle yard', and there was indeed a Norman Motte and Bailey castle here, perhaps built upon the site of an earlier fortification. Between The Bayle and the current site of the parish church, a substantial collection of monastic buildings once existed. Although there had been a priory much nearer the cliff edge in much earlier times, its successor had been relocated to around the current churchyard area around 1420. The extent of the buildings is clearly visible on a map of 1625 but have now long gone. However, the former home of the Prior of Folkestone still exists at Nos 1 and 2 The Bayle, next to the churchyard, and is still called 'The Priory'. This is now divided into individual flats but was described in 1535 by Henry VIII's commissioner as a 'neat, well kept house'. From 1818 to 1851, this fine old house was the home of local vicar Thomas Pearce. Pearce kept a school for young gentlemen and among his pupils in 1833 were the two sons of the artist John Constable. At the rear of this house can be seen an attractive turret feature that was added in the 1890s.

4. The British Lion (c. 1460), 10 The Bayle, CT20 1SQ

This Grade II-listed public house claims to be Folkestone's oldest and to date to around 1460 when it was allegedly known as The Priory Arms, being next to the old buildings of the Folkestone Priory. Though no documentary evidence to support this has been found,

The British Lion, reputed to be Folkestone's oldest pub.

Left: Pub sign of the British Lion.

Right: Welcome sign and a golden lion at the British Lion.

part of the wall of the old priory was found by local historian Eamonn Rooney in 1995 in the next-door cottage that is now part of the pub's premises.

Inside the pub is a small room, a 'snug', called 'The Dickens Room'. It is said that Charles Dickens used to like and use this room when he visited the pub during his stays in Folkestone in the 1850s. In 1855, Dickens stayed for three months in a house around the corner near the start of The Leas. Here, he wrote some of *Little Dorrit* and also wrote of Folkestone and the surrounding countryside in a publication called *Household Words* in which he referred to the town as 'Pavilionstone'.

Outside the pub sits an impressive stone lion painted gold, of uncertain age and origin, one of the many 'lions' in the form of pictures and ornaments to be found around the premises.

Today, the British Lion continues as a popular venue well known for its good home-cooked food and a range of real ales.

5. Sandgate Castle (1539), Castle Road, Sandgate, CT20 3AL

This is one of the five castles built along the south-east coast on the orders of Henry VIII in 1538–39. These all had a unique design that, if seen from above, resembled a Tudor Rose. The other castles in the series are at Camber, which stands in a remote position in a lonely field; Walmer, which is open to the public, is well known for its fine gardens

Above: Sandgate Castle, seen from the front entrance.

Below: Sandgate Castle, seen from its seaward side. The circular room is a recent addition.

Sandgate Castle and its surrounding grounds. The Martello Tower style of the central keep is particularly evident.

and is the official home of the Lord Warden of the Cinque Ports (the Cinque Ports is an ancient association of ports along the Kent and Sussex coastline); Deal, which is an English Heritage property and probably the best example of this type of castle; and Sandown, which is the most minimal ruin, most of it having succumbed to coastal erosion. These castles were all built in expectation of an invasion from France authorised by the Pope following Henry Vlll's split with the church authorities in Rome.

Sandgate Castle was built from stone quarried from the old Folkestone Priory and further adapted in 1805–06 to make its central keep more like a Martello Tower (of which more in the next entry) when England was once again under threat of invasion, this time by Napoleonic France.

In the mid-nineteenth century, the central Martello-style keep was used as a military prison, but after that the castle gradually fell into a ruinous state due to erosion by the sea until extensive renovation work was carried out in the 1990s. Sandgate Castle then went through a period as a restaurant and function suite until it was sold for use as a private residence, a role that it continues to fulfil today. An impressive cupola has been added to the top of the tower, as can be seen in these photographs.

6. Martello Towers (1805–06), eight buildings from East Wear Bay to
   Hospital Hill, Sandgate, postcode for Martellos 1, 2 and 3 is CT19 6PU

There are eight Martello Towers within the area covered by this book, so I have treated them as a single entry. They were originally built in 1805–06 as a defensive measure against expected Napoleonic invasion. Each one was composed of half a million bricks and had extremely thick walls – 8 feet thick on the landward side and an astonishing 13 feet thick on the seaward side from where an attack might be expected. Atop each tower was a cannon that rotated around the tower on a rail and was able to fire a 1lb shot for a mile. Each tower could house twenty-four soldiers and an officer but were never really manned like this as the threat of invasion passed away after the Battle of Trafalgar. In the ensuing years these towers have been pressed into use in various roles.

The Martello Towers are all numbered (there were seventy-four along the south coast). Numbers 1 and 2 are at East Wear Bay and are now private residences.

Number 3 on the East Cliff was used by the Royal Observer Corps in the Second World War and became a museum and visitor centre in 1989 before finally closing in 2004 (I worked there as a custodian for five summer seasons) and was briefly occupied for a few months by the Coastwatch Institution. Number 4 is in a private garden, and covered in ivy, at the western end of The Leas. It forms part of an artwork (parts of the Folkestone Artwork display around the town). Number 5 is derelict and situated in the grounds of a girls' school. Number 6 is derelict but is attractively situated next to a footpath in woodland behind Sandgate, while Number 7 is derelict and in the grounds of the army camp at Shorncliffe.

Finally, Number 8 is a well-converted private residence at the top of Hospital Hill, above Sandgate.

Anyone wanting to look around inside a tower as it would have been when first built and operational can visit Number 24 just down the coast at Dymchurch, which is open to the public by arrangement or on special open days. It is owned by English Heritage.

Martello Tower Number 3, atop the Cop and Point hillock.

Above: Martello Tower Number 6, hidden in the woods behind Sandgate.

Right: Martello Tower Number 2, a holiday let among the trees.

7. Folkestone Harbour (1809), Seafront, CT20 1QH

Folkestone's medieval harbour probably existed in the Tontine Street/Mill Bay area, but this had long gone before it could be documented. Many ideas and attempts at harbour construction nearer to the present site of the facility never came to fruition, but then a useable harbour was finally built in 1809. The harbour wall/breakwater for this was constructed by Thomas Telford and is today known as the East Head. This is constructed from large blocks of greensand and is very effective at breaking the force of storm-driven water against it while allowing water to flow back out between the rocks of which the wall is composed.

In 1842, this harbour was bought by the South Eastern Railway, who had been delayed by geological problems between Folkestone and Dover from driving through their proposed London–Dover railway. Taking advantage of the availability of the harbour, they quickly developed this facility and had a branch line run from Folkestone Central Station down to Folkestone Harbour by 1844. At first this carried coal, but from 1849 passengers were carried to the port, which became a popular gateway to the continent. Paddle steamers carried some 49,000 people across the Channel to Boulogne in 1849 alone.

The long curved harbour wall, currently known as the 'Harbour Arm', was completed in 1905 along with the lighthouse at its end. This catered for the much larger ferries of later times.

Folkestone Harbour played a very important role as the main port of embarkation during the First World War when some eight million troops are said to have passed through on their way to the battlefields of the continent.

The 1809 Harbour wall known today as the East Head.

Right: Harbour Railway Station
(now derelict).

Below: Detail of the 1809 Harbour wall
with the 1905 Harbour Arm and lighthouse
visible beyond.

In the 1970s, the harbour area was developed into a busy 'roll-on roll-off' car ferry terminal, but this closed with the coming of the Channel Tunnel. Today, the rail station has closed and the Harbour Arm has been turned into a pleasure pier with music, food and wonderful views.

The East Head, lighthouse and railway viaduct across the harbour are all protected by Grade II listing.

8. Foord Viaduct (1843), Foord Road, Bradstone Road and Bradstone Avenue, CT19 5AE

This spectacular structure has been described by architectural writer John Newman as the 'most exciting piece of architecture in the town'.

The Foord Viaduct was designed by Sir William Cubitt and built to carry the South Eastern Railway line across the deep valley at Foord (once a village, now absorbed as just a district of Folkestone), on its way from London to Dover. This massive structure has nineteen arches, each with a span of 30 feet and stands 88 feet high. Anyone who doesn't like heights is not advised to look down from their railway carriage when crossing the viaduct. It can be viewed from below at either Foord Road, Bradstone Road or Bradstone Avenue, which all pass beneath it. The Foord Viaduct is Grade II listed and kept in good repair as an essential piece of infrastructure.

Foord Viaduct, seen from Foord Road.

Foord Viaduct towers over the houses of Bradstone Road.

9. The Toll House (1847), Lower Sandgate Road, CT20 2JP

In 1784, a landslip created a shelf between the sea and the cliff edge below what is now The Leas. The Lord Radnor of the time decided to run a road along this, connecting Folkestone with Sandgate to the west. A wooden house was erected at the point where tolls would be collected but soon fell into disrepair.

With the coming of the railway and the successful development of the harbour, it seemed this route would be well used. The Radnor Estate, who owned much of the land around Folkestone, commissioned architect Sidney Smirke to work on various projects for them, one of the early ones being to design a new stone Toll House on the Lower Sandgate Road, which was subsequently built in 1847.

In 1913, the Lower Road, as it became known, was leased to the local authority, which developed it as parkland by the sea during the 1920s. Tolls were still collected for the Radnor Estate until 1973 when the rate for passage of a motorcar was 10d, a motorcycle 2d and a bicycle a halfpence. The Toll House was sold as a private dwelling in 1980 and the coastal strip of parkland fully developed into the beautiful and relaxing Lower Leas Coastal Park in 2000–01. Here there are three different zones: a 'formal zone' with laid-out gardens, seating, sea views, etc.; a 'fun zone', where a cave-riddled zigzag path winds down to an entertainment; and a children's adventure area. From the Toll House westwards, the scenery is greener and wilder, woodland and grassy banks with seating and barbeque areas, ideal for picnics.

The Toll House meanwhile sits comfortably in this idyllic environment between woodland and sea.

The Toll House undergoing roof repairs, seen from The Leas above.

The Toll House by the old Toll Gate, Lower Sandgate Road.

The Toll House in its idyllic woodland position above the sea.

10. The Wedge (1848), 75–81 Tontine Street, CT20 1JR

The Wedge is the modern name for the attractive building of that description at the western end of Tontine Street. Tontine Street was thought of as a great achievement back in the nineteenth century. Where a medieval harbour had earlier given way to an open stream, lined either side by hovels prone to flooding, there was now a street full of shops. Dickens in *Household Words* said of Tontine Street that it was full of shops, 'the business for which is expected to arrive in 10 or 20 years'. The business did come through however, though the street did not boom until the 1890s when it became Folkestone's main shopping street. The street itself was planned by Sidney Smirke in 1848, but why choose the name 'Tontine' you may ask.

The word 'Tontine' (to rhyme with 'chime') comes from Lorenzo Tonti, a seventeenth-century Neapolitan banker. A 'tontine' is a financial scheme by which subscribers to a common fund each received an annuity during their lives. As each subscriber dies, their share goes to the remainder until eventually the last survivor enjoys the whole income.

The Wedge was one of the later buildings to be finished but made a fine, large emporium well-suited to its role as a gentleman's outfitter/tailor/hatter run by Mr T. Logan from 1883 to 1893 when he went bankrupt and sold out to Mr R. G. Wood. Wood continued to run the business and employed Logan as his manager. Logan, along with his job at the outfitters, started a radical newspaper called *Folkestone Up To Date* that championed the causes of the 'working men, struggling tradesmen, oppressed cabmen and brave fishermen'. The paper ran from 1894 to 1904.

The Wedge, Tontine Street, today.

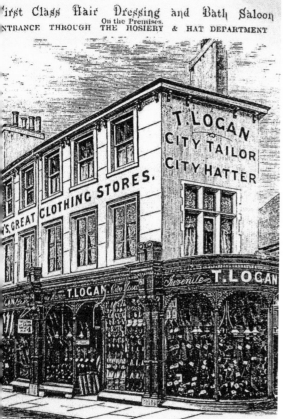

The Wedge in the 1880s/1890s.

New protective ironwork around The Wedge, 2015.

The Wedge still hosted a gentleman's outfitters business in the 1960s when I first came to Folkestone. In 2004, it became one of the first properties purchased by the Roger De Haan Charitable Trust for renovation and letting to creative individuals and businesses as part of a drive to develop a 'Creative Quarter' in this part of Folkestone. As part of continued improvements, a nice wrought-iron frontage was added to the curved western end of The Wedge in 2015. Today, the film company Screen South occupy the ground floor with flats above.

11. The Guildhall (1849), 42 The Bayle, CT20 1EJ

In 1848, Lord Radnor granted to Thomas Maycock of Broadmead Farm a lease on land in The Bayle in order to open a 'superior public house'. This building was then designed by none other than the noted Victorian architect Sidney Smirke, who was obviously very busy at this time.

This public house actually started out as The Globe and was only renamed The Guildhall in 1987 as the licensees taking over from them had previously run The Guildhall Tavern that existed next to the Town Hall in Guildhall Street and decided to bring their old pub name with them.

At one time, a long time ago, there used to be a small cannon in the courtyard at the front of The Guildhall. It is said that teeth used to be pulled in this pub and that the cannon was fired to drown out the screams of the amateur dentist's victims, or so the story goes.

Today, this spacious public house does a steady trade and offers a good choice of real ales, but no dentistry!

Above: The Guildhall public house, seen from the west.

Below: The Guildhall pub, seen from Bayle Street.

12. The Town Hall (1860), 1/2 Guildhall Street, CT20 1DY

This fine imposing civic building fronted by substantial Corinthian columns was designed by Joseph Messenger in 1856 and finished in 1860 by Whichcord and Bloomfield, who modified the design of the ground floor after a partial collapse during construction. The finished structure was opened as a Town Hall with a police station, a courtroom and, in the basement, a six-cell gaol.

The gaol's first inmate was Thomas Hart, who was arrested after breaking into his own home having been locked out by his father. Other examples of those 'sent down' here not long after the gaol's opening include 'a rollicking looking north country man who appeared at the bar without coat or waistcoat', on 6 January 1862. He was charged with being drunk and incapable – a regular occurrence then as now. Another 1862 report tells of 'a battered garrulous old woman' found guilty of 'uttering obscene language' and fined 5s, 'upon which she thanked the court and hobbled off'.

Civic administration from the Town Hall continued until 1967, after which a succession of shops, such as Superdrug and Waterstones, occupied the premises. However, with the setting up of Folkestone Town Council in 2004, a suitable base was sought within the town and when the old Town Hall became available again, the building was converted back to fulfil its former civic function, but without a gaol this time!

Left: The Town Hall today, seen from Sandgate Road.

Right: The back of the Town Hall building.

Inside the Silver Screen cinema, above the Town Hall.

As well as being a centre for local government administration, the Town Hall is a community space used regularly for exhibitions, lectures or meetings. A tourist information facility has been introduced, and a new town museum is planned to be opened in 2017.

On the upper floors of the Town Hall building is Folkestone's cinema, the Silver Screen, which shows all the latest films in traditional cinema surroundings and has done since opening in 1990. On Thursday mornings, the cinema hosts the Folkestone Classic Film Club, which has an interesting programme of those films you may want to see again having already 'been and gone' and others that are not considered mainstream. One unusual feature of the Silver Screen cinema is the red-velvet double 'love seats' at the back of the theatre where people can enjoy the film in close proximity with their sweetheart.

The Town Hall is a Grade II-listed building.

13. St Peter's Church (1862), The Durlocks, CT19 6AL

This interesting little ragstone church was established in 1862 for the fishing community around the harbour that had previously used the parish church along with the 'great and good' of the town. Local legend tells us that the latter objected to the odoriferous presence of the former, so that it was decided that the fishing folk should have their own place of worship, subsequently known as the Mariners Church and dedicated to the patron saint of fishermen, St Peter. Ten years later, St Peter's school for the local fisherfolk children was opened. Both church and school are very much in use today and are really not much changed.

Above: St Peter's Church, also known as the Mariners Church, on the Durlocks.

Right: St Peter's Church, seen from the east.

Statue of St Peter above the church entrance.

St Peter's has had its share of controversy having always been very much 'High Church' – the Oxford movement that began in the 1830s and sought to reintroduce many of the traditional trappings more associated with the Roman Catholic Church into Anglican places of worship and service. This led to a court case in 1872 known as the Folkestone Ritual Case. The vicar in charge, Revd Risdale, had to back down, but today it all seems academic as most of these practices, crucifix, stations of the cross, flowers, candles and incense are back as they are at both St Mary and St Eanswythe's and Holy Trinity Church. Both of these churches are also very much of the 'High Church' mould as a result of the famous or infamous Revd Matthew Woodward during his time at the Parish church between 1851 and 1898.

Another significant event in St Peter's Church's history was the terrible fire of July 1996 that resulted in the church being closed for two years. Three young men were arrested for arson; they claimed to be Satanists.

Today, at least at the time of writing, St Peter's is not torn by controversy nor disturbed by dramatic events. One of the fathers, along with some of the congregation, did transfer to the Roman Catholic faith a few years ago, but St Peter's itself still has a somewhat Roman Catholic ambience and has a loyal local congregation. Every 29 June on St Peter's Day, or the nearest Sunday to it, the church hosts the Blessing of the Fisheries, a service that starts in the church and winds its way down to the fishing harbour, involving the local population along the way.

St Peter's Church is today in good repair and is Grade II listed.

14. Holy Trinity Church (1868), Sandgate Road, CT20 2HQ

This monumental church is considered a prime example of Victorian Gothic architecture. It was designed by Ewan Christian and was built in 1868 for Viscount Folkestone as part of the Radnor Estate's plan to have a substantial church within easy walking distance of anyone living in the West End of Folkestone. Other examples of this policy being what is now the United Reformed Church near the Central Station and Christchurch, of which more in the next entry.

Holy Trinity Church itself was built of brick and Kentish ragstone with Bath-stone dressings and presents a wonderfully spacious interior with exceptional stained-glass windows. The church can seat up to 800 and was said at the time it was built to be 'one of the finest religious structures in the country'.

During the latter part of the nineteenth century, when the parish church of St Mary and St Eanswythe and St Peter's were both taking a decidedly 'High Church' direction, Holy Trinity took a different route. Guidebooks and directories of the 1870s and 1880s describe Holy Trinity as being neither 'High Church' nor 'Low Church' but 'Broad Church'.

One little-known claim to fame is that in the 1920s Holy Trinity became the first church in England to broadcast services by radio. The church became famous across the country for this innovation at the time. No doubt the fine acoustics created by this building led to its being chosen for this experiment.

Holy Trinity Church today appears to be in a very good state of repair and is a Grade II-listed building.

Holy Trinity church in Sandgate Road.

Left: Holy Trinity Church in Sandgate Road.

Below: Inside Holy Trinity Church.

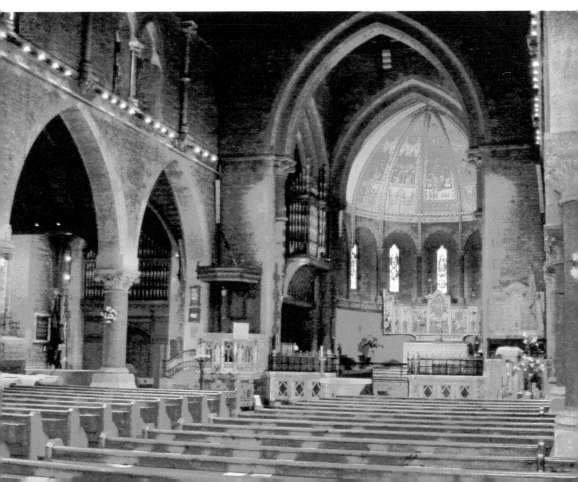

15. Christ Church Tower (1869), Corner of Sandgate Road and Manor Road, CT20 2BX

Christ Church was originally constructed in 1850, another example of the work of Sidney Smirke, but the tower was added only when the church was enlarged in 1869. As this is all that now remains following the destruction of the rest of the church by enemy bombing on 17 May 1942, I have concentrated on that.

Christ Church Tower is a Grade II-listed building and is graced with some unusual features. Protruding from the top of the tower can be seen some fine stone dragons. Around the clock face is an inscription with the stern message, 'TRIFLE NOT THY TIME IS SHORT'.

Where the main body of the church once stood there is now a Garden of Remembrance that has many plaques and memorials to military and other personnel, and most recently, the newly installed Gurkha Memorial, a tribute to those brave Nepalese who form an important element of the British Army and who are based, among other places, at Folkestone's Shorncliffe Barracks.

This sculpture by Rebecca Hawkins was unveiled by Joanna Lumley OBE on 4 October 2015. A small museum and visitor information centre about the Gurkhas, their history, culture and role in the British Army is sited in a converted Catholic Church in Shorncliffe Barracks, Cheriton.

Christ Church Tower stands alone in its Memorial Garden.

Above: There is a stern message around the clock face, Christ Church Tower.

Left: Gurkha statue in Christ Church Memorial Garden.

16. The Samuel Peto (1874), 23 Rendezvous Street, CT20 1EY

The first Baptist church on this site was built in 1845 and was funded by railway engineer, Baptist and Folkestone MP at the time Samuel Peto – hence the current name of this establishment. Peto incidentally was also responsible for Nelson's column in Trafalgar Square, London.

The first church here was known as Salem Chapel, but this was soon succeeded by the current building, which was built in 1874 by Joseph Gardner. It has an impressive, stuccoed, classical front with attached portico of paired Corinthian columns. The interior has been well preserved, retaining its chapel galleries, two pulpits and large organ.

The Baptist church sold the building in 1987, after which it was converted into interesting little shop units and renamed the Baptist Galleries. These closed in 1994, and the building was taken over by the Imagination Theatre, who used it for four years. Upon their departure, Wetherspoons purchased the building to convert into the current popular public house and eatery. Initially just known as Wetherspoons, the pub has subsequently been renamed The Samuel Peto and has continued to be a popular venue every day of the week.

The Samuel Peto main entrance in Rendezvous Street.

Stunning interior views of The Samuel Peto.

The Samuel Peto is a Grade II-listed building and the comfortable 'snugs' with books and historical information panels along with the stunning interior, wrought-iron stairways, stained-glass windows, wall and ceiling paintings, two pulpits and large organ continues to 'wow' first-time visitors with its magnificent ambience.

17. Old Post Office/KFC (1880), 88 Sandgate Road, CT20 2AA

This Grade II-listed building in Folkestone's busy main shopping street, Sandgate Road, was built in brick and limestone as the town's General Post Office. A royal coat of arms can be seen on the front gable, though much eroded.

The Post Office moved to new premises in 1937, and No. 88 Sandgate Road became the town's Labour Exchange, then Employment Office until that in turn moved to new premises at Palting House, Trinity Road, in the early 1970s. The old Labour Exchange/Employment Office building was thought of as very austere by many of those unfortunate to have to 'sign on' there. Apparently, the counters inside were very wide so as to stop disgruntled customers from climbing over them. When unemployment was high, particularly in the winter months, queues stretched all the way round to the bus station in Bouverie Square.

For some years now, No. 88 Sandgate Road has been an outlet for KFC. The interior of the building has changed somewhat, as you might expect, but the outside has been preserved, as can be seen on the photograph.

Old Post Office at No. 88 Sandgate Road, now KFC. *Inset*: Royal coat of arms (much eroded) under gable.

Above: St Andrews, once a convalescent home, now flats.

Left: St Andrews Chapel, attached to the former convalescent home.

18. St Andrews (1882), The Durlocks, CT19 6AL

St Andrews, designed by Ewan Christian, was built as a convalescent home with the attached church-sized 'chapel' added in 1889. The home was run by Sisters of the Community of St John the Baptist, an order of Anglican Augustinian nuns founded in 1849. Also known as the Clewer Sisters due to their order being founded at Clewer, near Windsor, the nuns helped in the poorest districts. Locally, this meant working with the churches of St Peter's, St Michael's and St Saviour's and with local schools. The sisters ran a soup kitchen, a crèche and collected clothes for the needy.

St Andrews was probably the nun's most lasting achievement locally. The convalescent home had six floors, 100 rooms and a lift. A few beds were kept for Folkestone residents, but mostly the care was for the poor from large towns needing sea air and good food to help their recovery from debilitating conditions.

The main building of St Andrews has now been converted into quality flats, while the church next door, which had been for use by both convalescing and the nuns themselves, is now used as the school dinner hall by pupils of nearby St Peter's School. The whole building complex of St Andrews now has a Grade II listing.

19. Former Volunteer Fire Station and Reading Room (1884), 51 Sandgate High Street, Sandgate, CT20 3AH

An unusual little building in Sandgate's interesting High Street, this was once the local fire station, the bright doors indicating where the fire engine was stationed. The attractive

Old Volunteer Fire Station, Sandgate High Street.

pointed tower atop the building housed the station's bell that presumably would summon the volunteer firemen from around Sandgate in the event of a fire needing attention.

The old fire station is today owned and maintained by the Sandgate Heritage Trust, who let the ground-floor engine room to the Sandgate Society. This serves as an information centre for the village, its history and local life, and is open on Saturday mornings to interested visitors. Above this, on the first floor, is a beautiful pine-panelled reading room with small bay windows overlooking the High Street. Next to the fire station is the weatherboarded Providence Inn, founded in 1843.

20. Folkestone Central Library (1888), 2 Grace Hill, CT20 1HA

Designed by Brightween & Bingon and opened by Sir Edward Watkin in 1888, Folkestone's Central Library and Museum, built in Queen Anne Renaissance style, was purpose-built to takeover from much smaller premises in the Old High Street that had been established by the Natural History Society when given a collection of local fossils by local historian S. J. Mackie.

The new library and museum was extended with the help of philanthropist Andrew Carnegie, to include what is now the Sassoon Gallery, named after the local MP who was also instrumental in fundraising for the venture.

Today, the library continues as ever but with the addition now of a 'Heritage Room' for local studies and research. The museum has been replaced in recent years by a History

Folkestone's main public library, Grace Hill.

The Masonic Hall, Grace Hill.

Resource Centre, but there are plans to create a new museum in the Town Hall by 2017. The Sassoon Gallery continues to host interesting art and historical exhibitions on a regular basis.

Across the road, the grey building with a grand-looking frontage including Ionic columns functions as the Masonic Hall and was designed by Reginald Pope and completed in 1880.

Both Folkestone Library and the Masonic Hall are Grade II-listed buildings.

21. The Catholic Church – Our Lady Help of Christians (1889), 41 Guildhall Street, CT20 1EF

This church, serving Folkestone's Catholic community, is known as 'Folkestone's Hidden Gem' according to the plaque on its frontage. The building was designed by architect Leonard Stokes and has today a Grade II listing. It is built in early Gothic style of local red bricks with Bath-stone dressings. The church has two towers, one topped with a copper bell housing. Between the towers is an impressive Gothic window, and around the towers' tops is a parapet battlement in stone, surmounted by a gable with a stone cross at its apex.

Inside the Catholic church is a magnificent ceiling with over 200 painted and gilded monogrammed bosses. There are a number of statues in the church, some of which were donated after the First World War by Belgian refugees who arrived in Folkestone during the conflict. The church remains popular with services often packed.

The Catholic church, Our Lady Help of Christians, Guildhall Street.

22. The Manor House (1893), 1 Earls Avenue, CT2c 3BH

In the late seventeenth century, the Bouveries, a Huguenot family, purchased a substantial area of land around Folkestone that had formerly belonged to Earl Godwin in the Middle Ages. In the early nineteenth century, the Pleydell-Bouverie's, as they had by then become, also acquiring the earldom of Radnor, decided to further develop their Folkestone estate starting with the establishment of the harbour in 1809. The West Cliff area of Folkestone was extensively developed from the 1820s onwards. The fifth Earl of Radnor had The Manor House built for him as a private residence in a prime position next to the greensward of The Leas in the early 1890s. This building, still known as the Manor House, is a wonderful structure of red brick and buff terracotta with an impressive entrance porchway, an attractive rotund, pinnacle tower at the western end, is half timbered around the outside of the top floor, and has enclosed gardens on the south side from where there are views across The Leas to the sea.

When the Manor House was first built, Lord Radnor had his own policemen patrolling the very exclusive Leas promenade, keeping order and good behaviour, if necessary, escorting off those inappropriately dressed, swearing or otherwise misbehaving. The Town Hall gaol had a number of inmates deposited there after being arrested for using foul language in a public place, including on The Leas.

During the First World War, the Manor House was used as a hospital for casualties evacuated from the continent. Today this fine building is Grade II listed and is divided into lovely flats, an ambience of exclusivity still evident.

Above: The Manor House, built as Lord Radnor's Folkestone residence.

Below: The Manor House, seen from the north-east showing the entrance porchway.

The Manor House, seen from the south side.

23. The Burlington Hotel (1893), 3 Earls Avenue, CT20 2HR

On the opposite side of the road to the Manor House stands another impressive building in red brick and buff terracotta and notable Dutch-style gables, as with many buildings in this part of Folkestone.

What is now The Burlington Hotel was originally started in the 1870s, but not completed until 1893, and formed part of the Manor Estates owned by the Earl of Radnor. The building was transferred to Burlington Mansions Ltd in 1946. During the 1960s and '70s, The Burlington was the premier four-star hotel in the area with its basement-level Bay Tree restaurant renowned locally and featuring twice in the prestigious Egon Ronay guide. During the Sunday carveries, diners had the pleasure of a harpist playing in the background. The 1980s saw The Burlington drop to three-star status but has seen considerable improvements since its purchase by the Sangiuseppe family in 1994 and is now considered to be a 'high-class three-star' hotel – so restoring its former prestige somewhat.

Right: The Burlington in red brick and buff terracotta.

Below: The Burlington Hotel, seen from the west.

24. Parade House, also known as Shangri-La (1894), 1 The Parade, CT20 1SL

This imposing terrace of flats looms over Folkestone Harbour with an ambience of great importance and significance. Likened by some to a Tibetan gompa, it is no surprise to find that the front part of the terrace, that you see from the harbour, has been named Shangri-La, the name of the hidden Himalayan monastery in James Hilton's 1933 novel *Lost Horizon*. The whole building is called Parade House and was built as an apartment block by W. M. Hoad in 1894.

Around the top of the building is eye-catching pargetting in blue and white depicting in carved figures various mythical creatures such as mermaids and sea monsters, and unpainted on the front of the building facing south-east, a large eagle-like bird, probably a griffin. This latter is probably responsible for the rumour that this was intended as a German Imperial Eagle and that this building was once, before the First World War, a German embassy. There are tales of séances being held in the cupola that surmounts the building and mysterious lights being seen from below. According to one of the local legends, this led to the police storming the cupola on one occasion where they found that the lights were Morse code signals being sent to German ships in the Channel and the 'séance', a meeting of German embassy staff. Another story tells of how one of the 'spies' was executed in the front garden.

Parade House looms impressively over Folkestone Harbour.

Above: A carved eagle can be seen below the cupola of Parade House.

Right: Impressive carvings of mythical creatures around the top of Parade House.

Certainly, the cupola in question would have made a good signalling base, and it was remarked in the press when Parade House was first built that a light seen in the cupola acted as a good (unofficial) beacon to guide boats into the harbour. Whether such an incident as described above ever happened is hard to say bearing in mind likely censorship in the year in question. What is certain, however, is that this was never a German embassy, consulate, legation or anything related, as has been confirmed by local historians and staff in the library Heritage Room, who have searched in vain in street directories of the time for any hint of these connections. The German Embassy in London has also been contacted and confirms that they have never had any connection with this building.

Never mind. The building itself is noteworthy enough by virtue of its striking appearance alone and can be viewed particularly well from the Parade Steps that lead up from the harbour to The Bayle.

25. Grace Chapel (1895), Grace Hill, CT20 1HE

Another very striking building, originally built as a technical school by Frank Newman of Folkestone. From near or far, this structure can't fail to impress with its pyramidal roof, pinnacles and crowning apex. A plaque outside tells how the foundation stone was laid by Stephen Penfold, mayor of Folkestone in 1895.

Grace Chapel at Grace Hill.

Since 1990, it has been known as Grace Chapel, or the 'Grace Independent Baptist Church and School' to give its full title. The Grace School is an independent Christian school for children aged five to fifteen. The building itself is now Grade II listed.

26. The Leas Bandstand (1895), The Leas, CT20 2DZ

Once, one of three bandstands in Folkestone, the other two, now long gone, being at Marine Gardens on the seafront and outside The Metropole on The Leas. The ornate ironwork is by James Allan and Son of Glasgow, and the whole structure has undergone thorough renovation in recent years following a campaign by the Folkestone Herald and funding from both Shepway District and Kent County Councils. The formal reopening of the bandstand took place on 15 December 2006, and this structure is now protected under a Grade II listing. The bandstand is used regularly in the summer months for band concerts and for the two-day multicultural festival that occurs every June.

There are a couple of interesting features in the vicinity of The Leas Bandstand, both on its seaward side. First, the 10-hour clock that tells the time in ten rather than twelve hours. This is based on an idea tried briefly in France following the revolution in the late eighteenth century and appear here as an 'artwork' courtesy of the Folkestone Triennial

The Leas Bandstand, now fully restored.

that brings contemporary artwork to the town every three years, many of which remain after the festival. The ten-hour clock remains from the 2011 Triennial. Immediately behind the ten-hour clock is the zigzag path that winds down to the Lower Leas Coastal Park through a series of grottoes and caves made of a special conglomerate called 'Pulhamite' – after its inventor, a Mr Pulham. This resulted from a job-creation scheme in the 1920s and the path and its rocky surroundings continue to be well maintained today.

27. The Metropole (1897), The Leas, CT20 2LU

A vast and monumental construction in red brick and buff terracotta topped by an impressive copper dome, overlooking The Leas. Designed by T. W. Cutler, The Metropole started life as a hotel and was the first large building in Folkestone to be lit by electricity, which the borough council supplied from 1896 onwards. Always considered a prestigious place, it once had a bandstand outside on the greensward, and various films have been made here over the years. These include *Lady Godiva Rides Again*, a 1951 film starring Dennis Price in which Diana Dors made one of her early appearances.

In 1960, the Hotel Metropole became the New Metropole, and in 1961, the New Metropole Arts Centre was opened, the rest of the building being given over to the development of quality apartments. Artist John Eveleigh was for many years the director of the New Metropole Arts Centre, which hosted many interesting exhibitions, literary festivals and other events over the years until its closure in 2008.

The monumental Metropole on Folkestone's Leas.

Above: The Metropole's impressive copper-domed top.

Below: The Metropole, seen from the south-east.

The other public areas of the New Metropole included a bar area and large conservatories. These were used over the years variously as a restaurant, bar/clubroom and a health centre/gym. Today, this extremely impressive Grade II-listed building is occupied entirely by apartments.

28. Spade House, Now Trading as Wells House Nursing Home (1900), Radnor Cliff Crescent, CT20 2JQ

Spade House was designed by architect C. F. A. Voysey in his 'Cotswold Cottage' domestic style for the famous author H. G. Wells, who had moved to Sandgate for recuperative purposes in 1898. The builders were William Dunk Ltd, who started work in 1900, and Wells and his wife Jane moved into their new home in December of that year.

During the construction phase, Wells had many disagreements with the builder and designer along the way, perhaps the most well known is how he objected to Voysey wanting to install a heart-shaped letter box. Wells objected to wearing his heart so conspicuously, so Voysey compromised on the Spade design, the house, ever afterwards, becoming known as Spade House.

During his time here, H. G. Wells wrote some of his most famous works. *The First Men in the Moon* was published in 1901, followed by *The Sea Lady* (1902), *Kipps* (1905), *The War in the Air* (1908), *Tono Bungay* (1909), *Ann Veronica* (1909) and *The History of Mr. Polly* (1910) to name just a few.

Spade House, now the Wells House Nursing Home.

Above: Original Spade House nameplate still in situ.

Below: Blue Plaque commemorating H. G. Wells.

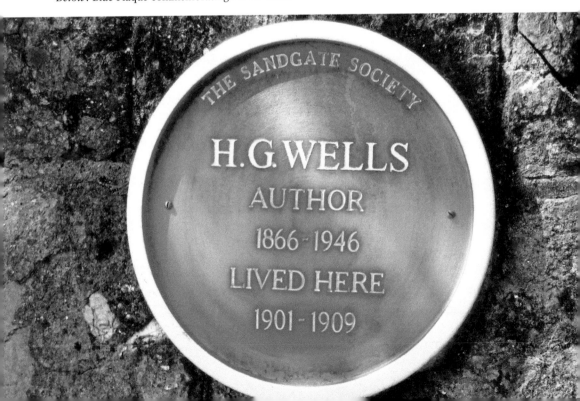

Spade House also became, for a time, virtually the literary hub of the Western world as many well-known writers visited Wells and quite a social circle developed around him. Among the better known were Edith Nesbit, Ford Madox Ford, George Gissing, G. K. Chesterton, Henry James, J. M. Barrie, Arnold Bennett, Stephen Crane, Joseph Conrad and George Bernard Shaw. However, in 1909, Wells was publicly embarrassed as a result of one of his many affairs, and he and his family moved first to London then to Essex for a quieter life.

Spade House meanwhile had a succession of private owners before becoming a vegetarian restaurant/hotel of some renown, once again attracting many famous names such as Yehudi Menuhin and Judith Durham of the folk group The New Seekers, as well as many other artists and musicians. In 1984, Spade House took on a new role as a nursing home, which it continues as today though now renamed Wells House Nursing Home.

29. The Leas Pavilion (1902), The Leas, CT20 2DP

Originally built as tea rooms to a design by Reginald Pope, this was once a very attractive building faced with buff terracotta and with a terracotta balustrade providing a decorative entrance at pavement level to a lower-ground-floor entrance to the main part of the pavilion. The internal venue is a spacious venue with a two-storey, galleried interior and sprung dance floor.

When opened, The Leas Pavilion was to be used exclusively for 'the highest class tea and refreshment trade with a view to securing the best class of visitor only'. In 1928, a stage was built as the pavilion was used as a theatre from 1929 until 1984. From 1929 to 1969,

The Leas Pavilion in its heyday.

Above: Interior of the Leas Pavilion, *c.* 1902.

Below: The Leas Pavilion (now derelict).

the theatre was home to the Arthur Brough players and hosted many entertaining plays and shows. Arthur Brough was best known for his role as Mr Grainger in the television comedy *Are You Being Served?* Although the Arthur Brough players moved out, the theatre was still used as such for many years – I went with a group of work colleagues in 1981 to see *Oh Calcutta* for instance.

In 1988, The Leas Pavilion once again became tea rooms as well as becoming a members' club that hosted a variety of stage performances. It was then renamed The Leas Club and continued successfully for many years, but finally closed in 2009.

This building is Grade II listed but has not fared well in recent years. Currently, the site is awaiting development around the outside and over the top of the old pavilion. The Pavilion itself is not part of this plan for flats but meanwhile is slowly falling apart with little sign of progress on the proposed surrounding development either at the time of writing. At present The Leas Pavilion presents a sorry sight indeed.

30. The Grand (1903), The Leas, CT20 2XL

Another impressive building that along with The Metropole dominates the western end of Folkestone's Leas. A fine building in red brick and buff terracotta topped by a copper-apexed cupola, The Grand was built between 1899 and 1903 by Daniel Baker as 'gentleman's residential chambers'. Many innovations were included in its construction

The Grand towers above The Leas.

Above: Inside Palm Court, also known as The Monkey House.

Right: The Grand's copper dome contains penthouse flats.

such as waterproof cavity-wall insulation, steel framing in-filled with reinforced concrete and suspended ceilings for improved soundproofing. Wall-to-wall carpeting was introduced as another novel feature.

The Grand almost instantly became the place to be and be seen. King Edward Vll was a frequent visitor, and he and his companions were often to be seen in the large sunlit conservatory at the southern front of the building. Locals would peer in trying to get a glimpse of the royal party. Since most of the men were quite heavily bearded, this practice became likened to looking at monkeys in a cage. As a result, the conservatory earned the nickname The Monkey House, which is still used for what is correctly known as Palm Court.

King Edward Vll often came down to Folkestone, not only with the queen but also his mistress Alice Keppel. It was suggested that the men in beards in the conservatory being humorously referred to as 'monkeys' were up to 'monkey business', which may be the origin of the term. The three-piece suits favoured by the king and his companions were referred to as 'monkey suits' – again a term originating, it seems, from goings on at The Grand. In 1909, the king opened a new ballroom with the first sprung dance floor in Europe. The first dance he took with the queen, and the second with Mrs Keppel.

During the First World War, the Belgian Royal Family took refuge in The Grand, which also served along with the Manor House down the road as a military hospital. After the war, Edward Vlll also came down to The Grand, as did Agatha Christie, where she wrote part of her famous novel *Murder on the Orient Express*. Later, in the 1950s, Princess Margaret used to visit and since then a number of television programmes have used The Grand as a location, along with others along The Leas.

Today, The Grand is a Grade II-listed building and has a mix of apartments, both privately owned and self-catering holiday lets, a thriving Palm Court and regularly it hosts art exhibitions and other events. The lower-ground-floor-level bar is known as Keppels and the accommodation is rated as three- to four-star. The copper dome surmounted by a union lag conceals penthouse accommodation with fabulous views across the English Channel. From the cupola apex beams out a Morse code light message of 'Earth Peace' installed by Yoko Ono in 2014 for that year's Folkestone Triennial.

31. Leas Cliff Hall (1927), The Leas, CT20 2DZ

The First World War and immediate aftermath created a pause in significant building developments around Folkestone, but by the mid-1920s the town seemed to be moving forward again.

The need for a large concert hall was met by the construction of The Leas Cliff Hall, designed by J. L. Seaton Dahl and opened on 13 July 1927 by HRH Prince Henry (George Vl's brother). This major venue has a pavement-level entrance with several storeys underground and an extensive lookout platform hanging over the cliff edge and shored up with mighty steel supports.

The Leas Cliff Hall continued to host band performances right through the Second World War and was probably thought quite safe being firmly embedded within the greensand cliff. The 1960s and '70s saw many big acts of the time play here: Donovan, Jethro Tull, KC and the Sunshine Band to name but a few, and of course the popular comedians. The 1980s saw the Yehudi Menuhin competition held here regularly and further improvements were

Above: The Leas Cliff Hall, seen from below.

Right: Statue of William Harvey, Folkestone's most famous son.

made to the hall in 1982, including the copper-topped octagonal pagoda-like entrance hall/café area.

Today, The Leas Cliff Hall remains a major focus for entertainment of all kinds as well as functions, conferences, exhibitions, election counts, etc. The Leas Cliff Hall is Grade II listed. Opposite the hall in Castle Hill Avenue is another feature of general interest – the statue of William Harvey, one of Folkestone's most famous former residents. It was he who discovered how blood circulates around the body and has, with some justification, been called the first medical scientist. The statue itself was created by A. Bruce Joy and was erected in 1881.

32. Former Burtons (1928), 24 Rendezvous Street, CT20 1EZ

In 1928, the menswear retail chain Burton had the Rose Hotel that formerly stood on this site demolished and a large retail store erected. The building is a good example of the architecture of the time and has been described as 'stripped classicalism' and seems to draw from both art nouveau and deco styles.

In the 1960s, Burtons moved to Queens House in Guildhall Street where, until 1962, the Queens Hotel stood. The company has since left the town, and their more recent shop is occupied by a branch of Bonmarché.

Detail of the top of Burton's building.

Burton's former building, Rendezvous Street.

Meanwhile, Burton's original building went through a chequered career with a snooker club occupying the first floor where Burton's staff 'recreational and rest rooms' were located, while downstairs there have been a succession of operators: Muswells restaurant (1989); Scruffy Murphy's, an Irish pub (1995); then in rapid succession, from 2000 to 2015 Fitzpatrick's, Mustang Sally's, Mustang's, The Zoo and most recently Kensi's. In 2016, at the time of writing, this floor of the building is being converted into use as a pizza restaurant.

Meanwhile, the snooker club continues as 'The Lanterns', and the exterior of the building has been left untouched – thankfully.

33. Debenhams (1931), 48–66 Sandgate Road, CT20 1DN

The provincial department store Bobby's moved into this building shortly after construction in 1931 and continued to trade here until 1972 when it was absorbed by the Debenhams group, who still use the building today.

The Debenhams building itself is in art deco style, typical of the time and according to the Folkestone Buildings Map 'matches classical, Aztec, Egyptian and other exotic forms to a suggestion of scientific streamlining and rationalism'.

Previous to the current building, an earlier low-level construction occupied this site and was used as a 'House Furnishing and Drapery' store by Adolphus Davis, who was mentioned by H. G. Wells in his novel *Kipps*, one of his best-loved books, published in 1905.

Debenhams extends beyond the 1931 building westwards into another older structure dating to the 1870s – an attractive building of red brick with turrets and copper domes.

Debenhams department store.

34. Coronation Parade (1935), Sunny Sands, CT19 6AB

In 1924, Lord Radnor gifted the East Cliff and Warren area to the people of Folkestone for recreational use. The area came under the care of the Folkestone Borough (now Shepway District) Council. Grazing by livestock was stopped on the Warren, access improved and facilities, such as beach huts and tea rooms, introduced. At the East Cliff, clifftop lawns and gardens were laid out (now partially lost to erosion) while rocks were cleared below the cliffs to create a sandy bathing beach (now known as the Sunny Sands). Behind this beach, a promenade was erected and subsequently improved in 1935, today known as Coronation Parade.

Within the promenade, which doubles as a sea wall, is a tunnel of archways passing through a succession of sea-facing arches so forming in effect a series of interconnecting changing rooms for those using the beach.

The Sunny Sands is very popular as a bathing and recreational beach and hosts events such as the Sandcastle Competition and Boxing Day dip. Dogs are banned in the summer months, and a lifeguard/rescue service operates from the promenade. Behind the western end of Coronation Parade is a large structure fronted by a terrace. This houses public toilets and the rescue/lifeguard base while within the structure, built in 2000, are contained part of Southern Water's mechanics for disposing of drain water from the town.

At the eastern end of Coronation Parade is another concrete structure housing within it equipment connected to the Cross Channel Interconnector that allows an exchange of electricity with France at peak times via an undersea cable.

Coronation Parade, seen across the Sunny Sands with mermaid artwork in the foreground.

Closer view of Coronation Parade.

Underneath the arches of Folkestone's Coronation Parade.

Coronation Parade is, at the time of writing (summer 2016), undergoing extensive renovation due to natural ageing taking its toll but combined with the need for safety reasons to repair damage to the promenade during Storm Imogen in early 2016. The beach, however, remains open.

35. Royal Mail Delivery Office (1937), Bouverie Square, CT20 1AA

This spacious and sturdy-looking building was designed by D. N. Dyke, built in 1937 and opened the following year as the General Post Office for Folkestone. This substantial increase in space from the much smaller premises around the corner at No. 88 Sandgate Road previously used allowed access to Post Office vehicles, the siting of a large sorting office and public counter area and even a staff canteen on the top floor.

The style of the building is classed as neo-Georgian, and a particularly attractive feature is the Portland stonework around the ground-floor windows and main entrance.

Immediately north of the old Post Office is another neo-Georgian site, the Folkestone Bus Station, though this was built later.

As for the old General Post Office itself, this is still a sorting and delivery office operated by Royal Mail but counter service for the public has moved around the corner to the local branch of W. H. Smith and is operated by Post Office Counters.

Royal Mail delivery office, Bouverie Square.

POST OFFICE

1937

Entrance to the former Post Office, Bouverie Square.

36. Coastwatch Lookout/Royal Observer Corps Post (1940 and 1958), Copt Point, CT19 6PU

Just to the east of Martello Tower Number 3 is a hilltop bunker of Second World War vintage, one of several in the vicinity, some connected to gun emplacements. This one was linked to Martello Tower Number 3 where a naval detachment and a Royal Observer Corp (ROC) post were based. It was run by the Admiralty and following the end of the Second World War lay empty for years. However, in 2004, the bunker was pressed into use as a base for the National Coastwatch Institution (NCI). The NCI is run entirely by trained volunteers who keep a watch for any vessel in distress, drifting inflatables or lilos, swimmers in difficulty, walkers falling down the cliffs or cut-off by the tide and other unfortunate accidents. They can summon the emergency services as appropriate and keep watch seven days a week from here. This branch of the NCI was awarded the Queen's Award for Voluntary Services by the Lord Lieutenant of Kent and presented to proud manager Tony Hutt at a ceremony on 7 October 2011.

In front of the NCI bunker, some strange concrete protrusions can be seen poking up through the turf. These belong to a former ROC post established around 1958 when the ROC were abandoning their former role of watching out for hostile aircraft to take on a new function measuring nuclear blasts, their location, plus wind direction and speed in the event of a nuclear attack. Training exercises were carried out regularly throughout the years of the Cold War. This and similar posts were in fact small nuclear bunkers, able to

Coastwatch bunkers with old Royal Observer Corps Post in the foreground.

Above: Former Royal Observer Corps Post at Copt Point.

Right: Close-up of what remains protruding from the Royal Observer Corps Post.

hold six ROC personnel for up to two weeks. They were equipped with bunk beds, dried food, water, filtered air supply and equipment to take the necessary measurements and relay these by landline onwards to the emergency services and functioning civil authorities, so that any necessary evacuation could be put in place and help and assistance for people and infrastructure be coordinated.

What we see today in the form of the odd-looking structures surviving are the entrance hatchway, an air-filter tower and fixture post for measuring equipment. This particular post was abandoned in the late 1960s due to concerns about coastal erosion and personnel transferred to work at other nearby ROC posts on the downs at Creteway behind the town and Ham Street, north of Romney Marsh. The ROC itself was disbanded in 1992 at the end of the Cold War.

37. The Civic Centre (1965), Castle Hill Avenue, CT20 2QY

As the years of post-war austerity faded into the past, new development picked up again, most obviously in the 1960s–70s timeframe, manifesting in the form of buildings of a different style not to everyone's taste. However, they are interesting examples of the architecture of the time, and some may come to be better thought of as time goes by.

The Civic Centre in Castle Hill Avenue is a nine-storey tower block housing the offices of Shepway District Council, which cover the areas of Folkestone, Hythe and Romney Marsh. This is the place that deals with council tax, housing benefit, refuse collection, local planning decisions, etc. The building itself combines aspects of modern and classical styles

The Civic Centre, Castle Hill Avenue.

The Town Arms on the Civic Centre.

and was opened for business by Princess Alexandra in May 1967. An additional three-storey reflective-glass building was added a couple of decades later.

High up on the wall near the front entrance to the building (which is a single storey fore-building) can be seen the Town Arms. These are topped by eagles like that on the front of Parade House (see earlier entry) and flanked on either side by the likenesses of St Eanswythe, the town's patron saint and Dr William Harvey, the town's most famous son and discoverer of the circulation of the blood.

38. Folkestone Police Station, Bouverie House (1966), Bouverie Road West, CT20 2SG

First, it's worth mentioning that Folkestone police station stands on an interesting site, building history wise. It was here that the Pleasure Gardens Theatre was built in 1886. This initially opened as the Folkestone Art Treasures Exhibition but closed after just five months, reopening not long after as the theatre. This impressive facility occupied 16 acres that included, apart from the theatre itself, extensive grounds incorporating gardens, tennis courts and facilities for hockey, croquet and skating. The theatre hosted shows, revues, musicals and concerts and later in the mid-twentieth century became a bit more like a nightclub. The Pleasure Gardens Theatre had the distinction on 29 June 1896 of having the first moving picture show in Kent. Over the years, the complex became rather shabby and not so well patronised. It finally closed in 1960 and was demolished in 1964 to make way for the current building, which was completed in 1966.

Above: The Pleasure Gardens Theatre in its heyday.

Below: Folkestone Police Station, Bouverie House.

Lone hawthorn tree survives from the days of the Pleasure Gardens Theatre.

In 1968, the Orion Insurance Co. moved into its new head office, having decentralised its operation from London. When I worked there (my first full-time job after leaving school), I was very impressed with this new modern building with its zigzag stairway and wonderful views from the top floor. Orion Insurance was superseded by Guardian Health in 1998, and their departure in 2000 saw the installation of the new Folkestone police station incorporating a new South East Headquarters for Kent Police. There has been an addition to this building since initial construction, an annexe at the front, added in around 1980. There is also one notable survivor from earlier days, a lone hawthorn tree on the lawn in front of the police station, all that survives from the days of the Pleasure Gardens Theatre.

39. Number One The Leas (1971), CT20 2DP

This was part of a development by the Radnor Estate of the eastern part of The Leas between 1969 and 1974. There were sea-facing flats along part of the road west of here as well as this striking building, originally constructed as office and retail space. Sainsbury's moved into the ground floor (now replaced by McDonalds, Iceland and other retail outlets), while the office space, then known as Fortune House, was occupied by the Welfare Insurance Co. from 1972. Welfare was another company decentralising its operation from London and for a while employed many office workers locally, but moved to Exeter in 1978.

Above: Number One The Leas, built as an office block, now flats.

Left: Number One The Leas, seen from below.

The yellow-brick tower of Number One The Leas, as it is now known, is 127 feet high and the building is spread over seven floors. The office space remained empty from 1978 to 1987 when it was converted into prestigious flats with stunning views over Folkestone, out to sea and along the coastline, particularly to the east.

40. The Grand Burstin Hotel (1975), Harbour Approach, CT20 2TX

Folkestone's first large hotel, The Pavilion, later The Royal Pavilion, was sited here in the 1840s. It was in this hotel that a Polish seaman stayed during the run-up to the Second World War while his asylum papers were processed. When accepted, he joined the Royal Navy and served with distinction. After the war, the gentleman concerned returned to the Kent coast and bought The Royal Pavilion Hotel, which was then owned by the Ministry of Defence, and initially, he turned it into a residential home. The man's name was Motyl Burstin.

In 1973, work commenced to demolish the old Royal Pavilion Hotel building and replace it with the current hotel designed by A. T. Bacon to look like a large, docked cruise ship. When the new hotel opened in 1975, it was called the Motel Burstin but has since been absorbed into the Britannia Hotel chain and is now known as the Grand Burstin.

The building itself is a huge fourteen-storey slab that must stand some 200 feet high and dominates the western end of Folkestone Harbour. Since its extension in 1982, the hotel really does look like one of the huge modern cruise liners that now regularly

The Grand Burstin Hotel, seen across the inner harbour.

Above and left: The 'Cruise Ship' appearance of the Grand Burstin is evident in these views.

call in at nearby Dover Harbour. Many local people detest this structure, saying it is not 'in keeping'. Is that really so though? Is the Burstin Hotel any more out of place in Folkestone Harbour than a cruise liner is in Dover? I feel sure that as time goes on the Burstin Hotel, as an example of 1970s architecture, will be much better thought of than it generally is today.

Whatever people think of the Burstin as a building, no one can deny it is a successful business and brings many visitors, especially coach parties to Folkestone. They seem to be arriving and departing incessantly and have not only a choice of bars and eating places within the hotel but a nightly cabaret that is different every night over a thirty-day cycle – you would have to stay over a month to see the same show twice! The Grand Burstin Hotel is Britannia Hotels group's most successful and as such must be regarded as an asset to the town.

41. The Saga Building (1977), Middleburg Square, CT20 1AZ

The Saga Building started life as Middleburg House, the last of Folkestone's big 1970s office blocks to be built, the demand for these having more or less evaporated during the years dominated by high inflation, political uncertainty and an energy crisis. The building remained empty for ten years until 1987 when Saga, the company that specialises in holidays and financial and other services for the over 50s, moved in.

The Saga Building, Middleburg Square.

Saga had started modestly many years earlier as a holiday company run from the seafront Rhodesia Hotel by its owner Sidney de Hahn. Its holiday business took off, and before long, the company had offices in Sandgate Road and eventually a head office in Middleburg Square. The business has continued to expand as we shall see, to become one of Folkestone's largest employers.

The Saga Building itself is a seven-storey office block designed by John S. Bonnington Partnership. It is particularly noted for its bronze-tinted 'glass curtain' walling. When it was first built, it was called Bouverie House and was nicknamed the 'coffee grinder' due to its tinted windows and walling resembling the tint of these devices at the time. When Bouverie Square became Middleburg Square, the office block changed its name accordingly (Middleburg was a continental town Folkestone was twinned with). Today, most people just know this as The Saga Building, which is what it now says above the front entrance. Meanwhile the name Bouverie House has moved up to the old 'Orion House', which is now the police station, as we have seen. If you're not local, this must all be very confusing!

42. Cheriton Parc, Former Channel Tunnel Customer Service Centre (1994), Cheriton High Street, CT18 8AN

The smooth lines of this fully glazed rectangular office building are designed in harmony with the Ashford International Station 16 miles west of here, rather than the less-striking

Cheriton Parc Saga Office, originally the Channel Tunnel Customer Service Centre.

Eurotunnel Terminal Buildings a quarter of a mile north. This three-storey building is attractively bowed at the entrance end under a bow-ended Belvedere and is a little reminiscent of the De La Warr Pavilion in Bexhill.

This part of the group of commercial buildings known as Cheriton Parc was designed by Nicholas Grimshaw and Partners as the Customer Service Centre for the Channel Tunnel Terminal but has, since 2008, been taken over by the ubiquitous Saga company as office premises.

A note about the address though: officially 'Cheriton High Street' Cheriton Parc is really far to the west of what is generally regarded as the High Street being beyond the large Tesco superstore almost in the countryside near the M20 motorway. You are not likely to pass it on the way to anywhere.

As modern buildings go, I find this one a particularly sleek and pleasing example.

43. Saga Headquarters (1998), Enbrook Park, Sandgate, CT20 3SE

To my mind, this is one of Folkestone's most impressive buildings, dominating the skyline landward of Sandgate High Street. This five-storey office building set on a hillside amid pleasant parkland resembles to me a great steel-and-glass castle. High towers at either end are stair turrets crowned by wind turbines and a viewing platform.

Saga Headquarters building at Enbrook Park, Sandgate.

Just to the west of this, overlooking the pleasant green of Enbrook Park, can be seen the vaulted roof of tented fabric that covers the Saga Pavilion, a marquee that can seat 800 under a row of broad-arched roof lights. This has sometimes been used for concerts and other events and also acts as the wonderfully light and airy canteen for the 1,000 or so Saga staff from the adjacent office building.

Both the Saga Headquarters building and Saga Pavilion were designed by Michael Hopkins and Partners in 1997–98 and were open for use from 1999. I worked there in the Travel Services Department during 1999 and 2000 and can honestly say I was awestruck by the cathedral-like interior of the headquarters building. It seemed almost like something from science fiction. I'm sure H. G. Wells, who 100 years earlier lived across the road at Spade House, would have approved.

44. Folkestone Academy (2007), Lucy Avenue, CT19 5FP

A spectacular three-storey school building designed by Spencer de Grey of Foster and Partners, this school can accommodate 1,480 pupils of secondary-school age and was built to replace the Channel High School with a new modern academy. The rotund timber-clad structure so obvious from the front of the building is a theatre for use by the school that specialises in the performing arts.

Being quite far from the main parts of the town, this wonderfully inspiring modern building is unknown to many, which is a pity since it deserves to be seen.

Folkestone Academy building at Lucy Avenue.

Above: The imposing Bouverie Place shopping centre building.

Below: Inside the Bouverie Place shopping centre.

45. Bouverie Place Shopping Centre (2007), Alexandra Gardens, CT20 1AU

After years of discussion and the demise of one plan for a shopping arcade, Folkestone finally saw its indoor shopping centre opened at Bouverie Place in 2007. The main building is a covered mall with connected open-air space. Most of the one side of the upper floors of the complex is occupied by a large ASDA store connected to a three-storey car park. Wonderful views across the town, coastline and downs can be seen from the top floor of the car park.

Within the mall area can be found many other familiar retail names such as Next, Primark, Peacocks, TK Maxx and New Look. Eating places include Starbucks, Cafe LaDelizia, Burger King and Subway.

Bouverie Place shopping centre architecturally has the appearance of a massive grey slab and dominates the way into the bus station and surrounding area. It may not be that popular aesthetically but certainly is on a more practical level.

46. The Cube (2008), Tontine Street, CT20 1SD

I can remember when the site of The Cube was occupied by a Congregational Church, but this was demolished in 1974 and made way for an office block known as Tontine House. This was initially occupied in 1987 by Eurotunnel then by Benhams, the first day cover specialists who changed the name to Benham House. When Benhams in turn moved out

The Cube, Tontine Street.

to occupy larger premises on an out-of-town industrial estate, the building was completely refurbished and included reflective windows, magenta paintwork and a bold new name – The Cube. Since 2008, when this makeover was completed, The Cube has served as the arts department of the local Adult Education Service and continues to be a popular venue for students studying a range of 'arts' subjects as well as occasionally holding art exhibitions for public viewing.

Atop The Cube can be seen a strange object in the shape of a headless chicken moving with the wind as a wind vane would. This is lit up with a blue light at night and is in fact an artwork called Whithervanes conceived by John Marshall and Cezanne Charles for the 2014 Folkestone Triennial, a tri-annual exhibition of contemporary art in Folkestone's public spaces organised by the Creative Foundation. This exhibit is one of these that have been selected to remain in the town as one of the Folkestone Artworks. There are similar Whithervanes at other sites around the town.

47. The Quarterhouse (2009), 45 Tontine Street, CT20 1JT

A three-storey, white-steel-clad building designed by Alison Brookes Architects and nicknamed the 'cheese grater' by some locals. Situated at the heart of Folkestone's Creative Quarter, The Quarterhouse contains a theatre and reception area on its ground floor, with seating for the theatre up to first-floor level where there is also a café/bar. The top floor contains the offices of the Creative Foundation. At night, the steel cladding is backlit, which enhances the look of the building.

The Quarterhouse, Tontine Street.

The Quarterhouse, seen from Payers Park.

The Quarterhouse theatre has seating for 250 people over two levels or standing capacity of 490 over the same area. It hosts a wide range of events from musical and comedy performances, films, presentations and meetings and in November of every year the Folkestone Book Festival.

The Creative Foundation, which is based on the top floor, is the organisation that since 2004 has been overseeing the development and management of the part of Folkestone's old town known as the Creative Quarter. Funded largely by the Roger De Haan Charitable Trust, the Creative Quarter has gradually developed rundown properties and let them at 'affordable' rents to creative businesses and individuals. Slowly but surely, this formerly rundown area has been transformed into something much more positive and welcoming, an eclectic and vibrant community and a much-improved built environment. In addition to the property development part of their remit, the Creative Foundation also maintains the Folkestone Artworks that are seen around the town and the three-yearly Folkestone Triennial exhibition that produces them.

Atop The Quarterhouse can be seen a metal water tower, one of several such constructions around Folkestone. These are all part of one of the Folkestone Artworks, using water towers to mark the course of the Pent Stream through the town to the sea. Cleverly called 'Pent Houses', the artworks were conceived and developed by artists Diane Dever and Jonathan Wright for the 2014 Folkestone Triennial.

In 2015, The Quarterhouse apparently won an award for being 'Folkestone's favourite ugly building', but then as we all know 'beauty is in the eye of the beholder'!

48. Rocksalt (2011), 4–5 Fish Market, CT19 6AA

Celebrity chef Mark Sergeant's restaurant by the harbourside was designed by Guy Hollands Architects to blend in with surrounding fishermen's huts and tan yard while exhibiting smooth lines and a contemporary appearance.

The restaurant and bar areas have a plate glass south side allowing as complete a view of the comings and goings in the fishing harbour as possible. The food, drink and service are renowned over a wide area. The restaurant specialises in using locally sourced food and fresh fish, exquisitely prepared and blended dishes complemented by an excellent range of fine wines.

Connected to Rocksalt is The Smokehouse, a quality fish and chip restaurant across the road with beautiful visitor accommodation above, in the heart of the bustling fish market area.

Rocksalt restaurant, seen beyond the harbour fountain.

Entrance to the Rocksalt restaurant.

49. Memorial Arch (2014), The Leas, CT20 2DP

A curved-steel memorial arch sponsored by the First World War commemorative charity Step Short. This was 'opened' by Prince Harry to much fanfare on 4 August 2014 to mark the centenary of the outbreak of the First World War, the conflict in which between 7 and 10 million (estimates vary) troops marched down what is now called the Road of Remembrance (previously Slope Road) on their way to the battlefields of the continent, many never to return. The arch stands at the eastern end of The Leas where the Road of Remembrance starts downhill towards the harbour. It was the order given to the troops marching down this hill to 'step short' because of the steep gradient that has given rise to the name of the arch's sponsoring charity.

The memorial arch itself caused some controversy due to its cost, but no one can doubt that it does make a striking memorial. The arch was designed by architects firm Foster Gearing and has been surrounded with a seating area with plaques behind the seats giving information relating to Folkestone's part in the First World War. The archway is lit up at night and forms the focus for related memorial events in the town.

A war memorial statue is situated just yards away, put up in 1922, and further west along The Leas, recordings of letters home by First World War troops are played from hidden speakers in the vicinity of the sea-facing seats of a viewpoint area. A square of 16,000 pebbles near the bandstand commemorates the first day of the Battle of the Somme, with a pebble numbered for each of those killed. This was placed here as part of the first Folkestone Triennial in 2008 and is now here permanently as one of the Folkestone Artworks.

Step Short Memorial Arch, The Leas.

Artist's impression of multistorey skate park due to open in 2017.

5c. Urban Sports Park (2017), Tontine Street, CT20 2DP

Another project by Guy Holloway Architects working with Maverick, a specialist skate park design consultancy. This is claimed to be the world's first multistorey skate park and is a £10 million project funded by the Roger De Haan Charitable Trust. The new building is expected to open in summer 2017 on the site of an old bingo hall demolished in 2015.

The new centre will accommodate skateboarding and scootering at beginner, intermediate and competition levels. There will also be state-of-the-art facilities for climbing, bouldering and boxing, including the potential for a new home for the Folkestone Amateur Boxing Club and a café, a rooftop space, a fountain room and thirty-two car parking spaces.

At the time of writing, this project is just getting underway but should have become a physical reality within months of the publication of this book. I therefore illustrate this final entry as I did the first, with an artist's impression.

Bibliography

Much of the information used in this book have been gleaned from having lived in Folkestone for most of the past fifty years and having written about it on many occasions. I did, however, refer to some specific books and booklets that proved helpful, and I list those here for the benefit of those who would like to read more.

Coulson, Ian (ed.), *Folkestone to 1500 – A Town Unearthed*, Canterbury Archaeological Trust Ltd, 2013.

Crawley, Simon, *Holy Trinity Folkestone*, in the Diocese of Canterbury, Holy Trinity Church, undated.

Easdown, Martin and Rooney, Eamonn, *Tales of the Tap Room*, Marlin Publications, 2000.

Edwards, Dame Eanswythe, *St. Eanswythe of Folkestone, Her Life, Her Relics and Her Monastery*, The Parish Church of St Mary and St Eanswythe, 1980.

The Grand, *The Grand – History*, privately published leaflet, undated.

Harris, Paul, *Folkestone – A History and Celebration*, The Francis Frith Collection, 2004.

Lunigair, Christopher, *Folkestone Map, A Guide to the Buildings in Folkestone and Sandgate*, Campbell Lumgain, 2010.

Nevill, Ann, *The History of Folkestone*, Anthony Rowe Publishing, 2009.

Newman, John, *The Buildings of England – Kent, North East and East*, Yale University Press, 2013.

Reader-Moore, Anthony, *The Parish Church of St. Mary and St. Eanswythe, Folkestone – A Brief Guide*, self-published, 2010.

Taylor, Alan, *Folkestone Past and Present*, The Breedon Books Publishing Company Ltd, 2002.

Taylor, Alan, *Folkestone Through Time*, Amberley, 2009.

Various, *Everywhere Means Something to Someone*, Strange Cargo, 2011.

Witney, Charles, *Folkestone – A Pictorial History*, Phillimore and Co. Ltd, 1986.

Acknowledgements

I would like to thank Drew Smith BA MIFA and Mikko Kriek MIFA for permission to use their fine images of what the Folkestone Roman Villa may have looked like in its heyday, Folkestone Town Council and designer John Sims for permission to use their town maps as the basis for those used in this book, Guy Holloway Architects for the use of their image of the projected Multistorey Skate Park/Indoor Sports Centre, Judith Hemmings for typing the manuscript, my partner Candida for help and advice along the way and John Webber for much-appreciated practical help.

About the Author

Paul Harris was born in Tunbridge Wells, Kent, in 1954 but has lived for most of the time since 1962 in the seaside town of Folkestone. When he left a long career in the Civil Service in 1997, he worked in a variety of heritage and tourism related roles until he eventually turned his long-term paying hobby of writing into a full-time occupation. He has, over the past thirty years, had some 500 articles published in a variety of local, national and international newspapers, magazines, compilations and anthologies. Paul has also had over twenty books published, many of a local-interest nature starting in 1993 with *Folkestone Warren in Old Picture Postcards* for the European Library through to his two previous titles for Amberley, *The White Cliffs of Dover* and *The Jurassic Coast*, published in 2013 and 2014, respectively.

Paul lives in Folkestone's growing Creative Quarter with his partner Candida. When not writing, he enjoys walking and observing nature around the local coast and countryside.

Also Available from Amberley Publishing

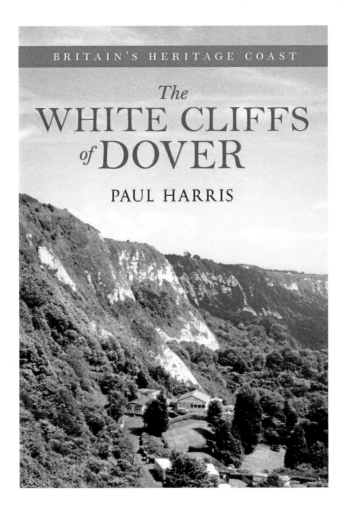

This fascinating selection of photographs traces some of the many ways in which Folkestone has changed and developed over the last century.

Paperback
180 illustrations
96 pages
978-1-848-1887-6

Available from all good bookshops or to order direct
please call **01453-847-800**
www.amberley-books.com